THE LITTLE
PASTA
COOKBOOK

THE LITTLE

PASTA

COOKBOOK

SMITHMARK

This edition first published in 1996 by
SMITHMARK Publishers
a division of US Media Holdings Inc.
16 East 32nd Street
New York, NY 10016

Produced by
Anness Publishing Limited
1 Boundary Row
London SE1 8HP

SMITHMARK books are available for bulk purchase for sales
promotion and for premium use. For details write or call the
manager of special sales, SMITHMARK Publishers, a division
of US Media Holdings Inc., 16 East 32nd Street, New York,
NY 10016; (212 532 6600)

ISBN 0-8317-7378-2
Publisher Joanna Lorenz
Senior Cookery Editor Linda Fraser
Assistant Editor Emma Brown
Designers Patrick McLeavey & Jo Brewer
Illustrator Anna Koska
Photographers Steve Baxter, Edward Allwright, Amanda
Heywood, David Armstrong, James Duncan & Karl Adamson
Recipes Sarah Gates, Steven Wheeler, Carla Capalbo,
Elizabeth Martin, Catherine Atkinson, Annie Nichols,
Shirley Gill, Maxine Clark & Norma MacMillan

10 9 8 7 6 5 4 3 2 1

Printed in Singapore by
Star Standard Industries Pte Ltd

Contents

Introduction

Singing the praises of pasta is rather like preaching to the converted; its popularity is phenomenal. Everyone loves pasta, from the young 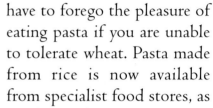 child enjoying spaghetti hoops to the pensioner looking for a nourishing meal that is quick to prepare. Struggling students live on pasta; families find it the perfect food for mid-week meals; lovers make a ritual of cooking and eating it together.

Pasta is convenient, easy to cook and very inexpensive. Composed largely of carbohydrate, it provides energy with very little fat. Marathon runners invariably dine on pasta before a big race. Slimmers find it filling, and it can form a very useful part of a calorie-controlled diet, so long as the sauces are sensibly selected. Nor do you have to forego the pleasure of eating pasta if you are unable to tolerate wheat. Pasta made from rice is now available from specialist food stores, as are pastas made from other grains, including barley, corn and buckwheat.

Dried pasta is an excellent pantry ingredient. It has a long shelf life, and it can swiftly be turned into a meal with a simple sauce based on canned tomatoes or tuna. Fresh pasta is now widely available, and as it freezes well, it is equally convenient.

Pasta comes in an amazing array of shapes, some of which are described on pages 8 and 9. From tiny stars for adding to soup to large shells for stuffing, there is a pasta shape for every occasion. Serve long, thin pasta with a good coating sauce, while twists, quills or shells can take something more chunky. Flat noodles make the perfect base for a creamy sauce.

Some pastas now have subtle flavorings. Spinach and tomato types have been around for some time, but the range has now been extended to include mushroom, asparagus, smoked salmon, chili, herb and the dramatic black pasta, which owes its color to squid ink.

It would be easy to overlook oriental pastas. There are so many of these that they could easily fill a cookbook of their own, together with the sauces and stir-fries that traditionally accompany them. For a taster, you could try Chinese egg noodles or cellophane noodles, Japanese shirataki or udon, or Thai rice flour noodles. Oriental noodles tend to cook very quickly, so it is vital that you follow the instructions on the package.

Whether you serve pasta with a simple butter or oil dressing, toss it with a sauce, use it in a savory bake or even a dessert, it is infinitely versatile. This collection of recipes proves the point, ranging as it does from tempting appetizers like Pasta with Shrimp & Feta Cheese to dishes for easy entertaining such as Tagliatelle with Pea Sauce, Asparagus & Fava Beans. Along the way, you'll meet some tasty old favorites, such as Fettuccine all'Alfredo, Spaghetti alla Carbonara and Macaroni Cheese. There are plenty of suggestions for vegetarians, and a tempting selection of simple pasta salads too.

7

Familiar Pasta Types

CANNELLONI
These large, hollow pipes are usually stuffed, topped with a sauce and grated cheese, then baked. Stuffed parboiled cannelloni can also be deep-fried.

MACARONI (MACCHERONI)
Although this pasta was originally sold as long, narrow tubes, somewhat thicker than spaghetti, the type most popular today is the little curved quick-cooking short-cut or elbow macaroni.

CONCHIGLIE
These shells come in various sizes, the largest being suitable for stuffing. Small ones are good for seafood salads.

FETTUCCINE
Often shaped into nests before packaging, these flat ribbon noodles are particularly good with cream sauces.

FUSILLI
These twists or spirals come in various lengths. The short shapes are good with chunky sauces.

LASAGNE
Rectangular sheets of pasta, these are layered with sauces for one of the most popular baked pasta dishes.

CAPPELLINI/CAPPELLI DI ANGELO
Long, very thin pasta that is sometimes dried in coils to keep it from breaking. It takes its name from the Italian word for hair, and the coiled form is also known as angel hair pasta.

MAFALDE
Ruffled edges give these flat noodles an interesting appearance when cooked.

RUOTI
Children like this wheel-shaped pasta.

SPAGHETTI

The name comes from the Italian word for string, a perfect description for the thin pasta strands. Spaghetti comes in a variety of flavors and colors: plain white, pink-red tomato, green spinach and brown whole wheat. You may also find the white, red and green varieties in mixed packets.

TAGLIATELLE

These flat ribbon noodles, made from egg pasta are usually dried in loose coils to prevent them breaking. A mixture of white and green tagliatelle is sometimes labeled as "paglia e fieno" (straw and hay). Like, the very similar, fettuccine, tagliatelle is best served with a creamy sauce.

FARFALLE

The word means "butterflies," and the shapes are also referred to as bows. They come in various sizes.

PENNE

Also known as quills, the term describes hollow pasta, cut on the slant into short lengths. Penne rigate is the ridged form.

TORTELLINI

These small, stuffed pasta shapes need little by way of accompaniment, and are best served with either a very simple sauce, or, more usually, just olive oil or a little melted butter. The plainer varieties are sometimes added to soup.

Techniques

HOW MUCH PASTA DO YOU NEED?

Allow 2–3 ounces per person for a starter; 4–6 ounces for a main course which also includes a sauce. If you cook more pasta than you need, rinse the surplus under cold water, drain thoroughly and toss with a little oil. Place in a bowl, cover and leave to cool completely, then chill and use the next day as the basis for a salad, or to add to soup.

COOKING

Bring a large saucepan of salted water to a rapid boil. Add the pasta, stir well, then reduce the heat to keep the water at a rolling boil without allowing it to boil over. Stir the pasta once or twice more during cooking to keep the strands or shapes separate. Dried pasta will require about 8–12 minutes, but fresh pasta cooks far more rapidly and some strands or shapes will be ready as soon as they rise to the surface of the boiling liquid. Filled fresh pasta will take up to 5 minutes to cook.

TESTING

Using a slotted spoon, remove a strand or piece of pasta from the pan. Squeeze it between your fingers. It should break cleanly. The well-known Italian term is *al dente* (to the bite), which means that the pasta should be tender while retaining a degree of texture. As soon as the pasta is ready, drain it thoroughly. If you merely turn off the heat and leave it in the water, it will continue to cook and will rapidly become flabby.

SERVING

Have ready a warmed serving bowl. A large deep bowl is best as it will hold in the heat and give enough room for tossing. Place a knob of butter or a little olive oil in the bowl, add the drained pasta and toss well. If you are adding a creamy sauce omit the butter or oil. If the sauce is chunky, it is a good idea to toss the pasta with a small amount of sauce, then serve it with the remaining sauce piled on top.

TIPS

• Use whole wheat pasta for extra fiber, but cook in plenty of boiling water and check it frequently when cooking as it may absorb more liquid than plain pasta.

• Many cooks swear by adding a dash of oil to the water when cooking pasta. It is not absolutely necessary, but does help to keep the pieces or strands separate and also makes it less likely that the water will boil over.

• Look out for special large pasta pans with integral strainers: the pasta is cooked in an inner, perforated pan which sits inside the main pan. This not only makes draining extremely easy, it also prevents the pasta from sticking to the bottom of the pan during cooking.

• When cooking spaghetti, push the strands gently down into the pan so that they curl into the boiling water as they soften.

• Uncooked fresh pasta freezes well and can be cooked from frozen, although it will take marginally more time. Baked pasta dishes like lasagne also freeze well, but plain cooked pasta is not an ideal candidate, as it can be limp and soggy when thawed.

Appetizers & Light Lunches

Pasta, Bean & Vegetable Soup

INGREDIENTS

¾ cup dried borlotti beans or black-eyed peas,
soaked overnight in water to cover
5 cups unsalted vegetable or chicken broth
1 large onion, chopped
1 large garlic clove, finely chopped
2 celery stalks, chopped
½ red bell pepper, seeded and chopped
14-ounce can chopped tomatoes
8 ounces piece of smoked bacon loin
2 zucchini, halved lengthwise and sliced
1 tablespoon tomato paste
¾ cup tiny dried pasta shapes for soup
salt and ground black pepper
shredded fresh basil, to garnish

SERVES 4–6

1 Drain the beans and peas, and put them in a large heavy-bottomed saucepan. Add fresh, cold water to cover. Bring to a boil, boil hard for 10 minutes, then drain the beans in a colander. Rinse the beans under cold water, return them to the pan, and add the broth. Bring to a boil, skimming off any foam that rises to the surface.

2 Add the onion, garlic, celery, red pepper, tomatoes and bacon (in the piece) to the pan.

3 Bring the liquid in the pan back to a boil, lower the heat, cover, and simmer for 1½ hours or until the beans and peas are tender. Lift out the bacon, shred it coarsely with two forks, and keep it hot.

4 Add the zucchini and tomato paste to the soup. Season if necessary, though it will probably be unnecessary to add salt. Simmer the soup for 5–8 minutes more, adding the pasta shapes toward the end of cooking so that they cook for no longer than the time suggested on the package.

5 Stir in the shredded bacon. Serve the soup in heated bowls, with a sprinkling of shredded basil on top of each portion.

13

Pasta with Shrimp & Feta Cheese

INGREDIENTS

4 cups penne or other dried pasta shapes
¼ cup butter
1 pound raw shrimp, peeled and deveined
6 scallions
8 ounces feta cheese, cubed
small bunch fresh chives, snipped
salt and ground black pepper

SERVES 4

14

1 Bring a large saucepan of lightly salted water to a boil. Add the pasta, and cook for 10–12 minutes or according to the instructions on the package.

2 Meanwhile melt the butter in a second pan, and add the raw shrimp. Cook over moderate heat for a few minutes until they turn pink. Slice the scallions, and stir in. Continue to cook gently for 1 minute more, stirring occasionally.

3 Add the feta cheese and half of the snipped chives to the shrimp mixture. Toss it all lightly together to mix, and then season with black pepper. When the pasta is just tender, drain it well, divide it among individual serving dishes, and spoon the sauce on top. Serve sprinkled with the remaining chives.

VARIATION
Try using another slightly salty cheese, such as Gorgonzola, in this dish.

Fresh Pea & Ham Soup

INGREDIENTS

1 cup small dried pasta shapes
2 tablespoons sunflower oil
6 scallions, chopped
3 cups frozen peas
5 cups chicken broth
8 ounces raw unsmoked ham or gammon
4 tablespoons heavy cream
salt and ground black pepper

SERVES 4

16

1 Bring a large saucepan of lightly salted water to a boil. Add the dried pasta shapes, and cook for 10–12 minutes or according to the instructions on the package, until it is *al dente*. Drain, refresh under cold water to avoid further cooking, and drain again. Set the pasta aside until required.

2 Heat the oil in a large heavy-bottomed saucepan. Cook the scallions for several minutes until soft. Add the frozen peas and the chicken broth, and bring to a boil. Lower the heat, and simmer for 10 minutes until the mixture becomes very soft.

3 Purée the soup in a food procesor or blender. Return it to the clean pan. Cut the ham or gammon into short fingers. Add these to the soup, and simmer until cooked. Stir in the pasta, and heat through gently for 2–3 minutes. Stir in the cream, season to taste, and serve in heated bowls.

Pasta Bows with Smoked Salmon & Dill

INGREDIENTS

4 cups dried pasta bows (farfalle)
¼ cup butter
6 scallions, sliced
6 tablespoons dry white wine or vermouth
scant 2 cups heavy cream
freshly grated nutmeg
8 ounces smoked salmon
2 tablespoons chopped fresh dill, plus a few
sprigs to garnish
½ lemon
salt and ground black pepper

SERVES 4

17

1 Bring a large saucepan of lightly salted water to a boil. Add the pasta, and cook for 10–12 minutes or according to the instructions on the package.

2 Heat the butter, and fry the scallions for about 1 minute. Add the wine, and boil it away to 2 tablespoons. Stir in the cream, and add seasoning and nutmeg to taste. Bring to a boil, then lower the heat, and simmer for 2–3 minutes until thickened.

3 Using a sharp knife, cut the smoked salmon into 1-inch pieces. Stir the pieces into the sauce along with the chopped dill. Squeeze in a little lemon juice to taste, and check the seasoning. Keep the sauce warm until you are ready to serve it.

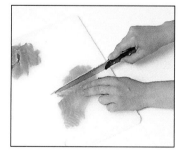

4 When the pasta is just tender, drain it well, toss it with the sauce, and divide among heated serving dishes. Serve garnished with dill.

Fettuccine all'Alfredo

INGREDIENTS

1 pound dried fettuccine
2 tablespoons butter
scant 1 cup heavy cream
½ cup freshly grated Parmesan cheese, plus
extra to serve
freshly grated nutmeg
salt and ground black pepper
dill sprigs, to garnish

SERVES 4

18

2 Meanwhile carefully melt the butter in ⅔ cup of the heavy cream in a large heavy-bottomed saucepan. Bring the mixture to a boil, then lower the heat, and simmer for about 1 minute until slightly thickened.

3 Drain the pasta well, add it to the cream sauce, and toss it gently over the heat until all the strands are well coated in the sauce. Add the rest of the cream, with the Parmesan, nutmeg and salt and pepper to taste. Toss again until well coated and heated through. Serve at once, topping each portion with extra grated Parmesan and a sprig of dill.

1 Bring a large saucepan of lightly salted water to a boil. Add the pasta, and cook for 10 minutes or for about 2 minutes less than the timing suggested on the package. The pasta should still be a little firm to the bite (*al dente*) – don't let it overcook.

COOK'S TIP
Fresh fettuccine will cook much more quickly than dried pasta, and is ready as soon as it rises to the surface of the boiling water. When using fresh pasta, cook it at the last minute, after making the cream sauce. Fresh fettuccine is available from most good supermarkets.

Spaghetti Olio e Aglio

INGREDIENTS

1 pound dried spaghetti
½ cup olive oil
2 garlic cloves
2 tablespoons chopped fresh parsley
salt and ground black pepper

SERVES 4

1 Bring a large saucepan of lightly salted water to a boil. Add the dried spaghetti, and cook for about 10–12 minutes, or according to the instructions on the package, until it is *al dente*.

2 Meanwhile heat the olive oil in a saucepan. Using a sharp knife, peel and chop the garlic on a chopping board. Add it, with a pinch of salt, to the oil. Cook gently, stirring all the time, until the garlic has turned pale gold in color.

3 As soon as the spaghetti is just tender, drain it well in a strainer, and return it to the clean pan. Pour over the warm – but not sizzling – garlic and oil, and toss gently until all the spaghetti strands are well coated. Add the chopped parsley along with plenty of ground black pepper and salt if required. Finally, thoroughly toss the spaghetti once more before serving.

Pasta Pronto with Parsley Pesto

INGREDIENTS

4 cups dried pasta shapes
¾ cup whole blanched almonds
½ cup slivered almonds
¾ cup fresh parsley
2 garlic cloves, crushed
3 tablespoons olive oil
3 tablespoons lemon juice
1 teaspoon sugar
1 cup boiling water
salt
¼ cup freshly grated Parmesan cheese, to serve

SERVES 4

1 Bring a large saucepan of lightly salted water to a boil. Add the pasta, and cook for about 10–12 minutes or according to the instructions on the package, until it is *al dente*. Preheat the broiler.

2 Keeping them separate, spread out the whole and slivered almonds in a broiler pan. Toast them until golden. Set the slivered almonds aside.

3 Chop the parsley finely in a food processor or blender. Add the toasted, whole almonds, and process to a fine consistency. Add the garlic, olive oil, lemon juice, sugar and boiling water. Process the mixture until well combined.

4 When the pasta is just tender, drain it well, and return it to the clean pan. Add half the sauce (the rest of the sauce will keep in a screw-topped jar in the fridge for up to 10 days). Toss gently to coat. Serve at once in heated bowls, topping each portion with a little of the grated Parmesan cheese and a few of the toasted slivered almonds. Extra grated Parmesan cheese can be served separately, if liked.

Vegetarian Dishes

Pasta with Spring Vegetables

INGREDIENTS

4 ounces baby leeks, trimmed
8 ounces asparagus spears, trimmed
1 small fennel bulb
4 ounces broccoli florets, cut into tiny sprigs
1 cup fresh or frozen peas
3 cups penne or other dried pasta shapes
3 tablespoons butter
1 shallot, chopped
3 tablespoons chopped fresh mixed herbs
1¼ cups heavy cream
salt and ground black pepper
freshly grated Parmesan cheese, to serve

SERVES 4

1 Cut the leeks and asparagus diagonally into 2-inch lengths. Trim the fennel bulb, and remove any tough outer leaves. Cut the fennel into wedges, leaving the layers attached at the root end so that the pieces remain intact. Bring two large saucepans of lightly salted water to a boil.

2 Cook all the vegetables separately in one of the pans of water. As soon as each type is tender, transfer it with a slotted spoon to a bowl. Keep all of the vegetables hot. Add the pasta to the second pan of boiling water. Cook for 10–12 minutes or according to the instructions on the package.

3 Melt the butter in a pan. Add the shallot, and cook until softened but not browned. Stir in the herbs and cream. Cook for a few minutes, until slightly thickened.

4 Drain the pasta well, pile it into a heated bowl, and add the sauce and cooked vegetables. Season, and toss to mix. Serve with the Parmesan.

23

Spinach & Ricotta Conchiglie

INGREDIENTS

12 ounces large dried conchiglie (shells)
scant 2 cups strained puréed canned tomatoes
10 ounces frozen chopped spinach, thawed
2 ounces fresh white bread crumbs
½ cup milk
4 tablespoons olive oil
1 cup ricotta cheese
freshly grated nutmeg
1 garlic clove, crushed
½ teaspoon black olive paste (optional)
¼ cup freshly grated Parmesan cheese
⅓ cup pine nuts
salt and ground black pepper

SERVES 4

24

1 Preheat the oven to 350°F. Bring a large saucepan of lightly salted water to a boil. Add the pasta, and cook for 10–12 minutes or according to the instructions on the package. Refresh under cold water, drain, and set aside.

2 Turn the canned tomatoes into a nylon strainer set over a bowl. Press it against the strainer to remove excess liquid, then scrape into a separate bowl. Discard the tomato liquid, or save it for adding to soups or sauces. Wash the strainer, and repeat the process with the spinach.

3 Place the bread crumbs, milk and 3 tablespoons of the olive oil in a food processor or blender. Process to combine, then add the spinach and ricotta cheese.

Process briefly, then scrape the mixture into a bowl, and add the nutmeg and salt and pepper to taste.

4 Add the garlic, remaining olive oil and olive paste (if using) to the tomatoes. Spread the sauce evenly over the bottom of a flameproof dish. Spoon the spinach

mixture into a pastry bag fitted with a large, plain nozzle, and fill the pasta shapes (alternatively, fill with a spoon), and arrange them over the sauce in the dish. Cover the dish with foil, and heat through in the oven for 15–20 minutes.

5 Preheat the broiler. Remove the foil, and sprinkle the Parmesan cheese and pine nuts over the filled conchiglie. Brown the topping under the broiler, and serve the dish at once.

Macaroni Cheese

INGREDIENTS

1½ cups grated Parmesan cheese or Cheddar,
or a combination
¾ cup fresh white bread crumbs
4 cups short-cut macaroni or other dried hollow
pasta shapes
Italian parsley, to garnish
BÉCHAMEL SAUCE
2 cups milk
1 bay leaf
3 mace blades
¼ cup butter
6 tablespoons flour

SERVES 6

1 Make the béchamel sauce. In a small saucepan, heat the milk with the bay leaf and mace until just below boiling point. Set aside to infuse for about 30 minutes, then strain.

2 Melt the butter in a saucepan, stir in the flour, and cook for 1 minute. Gradually add the flavored milk, stirring constantly until the sauce boils and thickens. Remove the béchamel sauce from the heat, stir in three-quarters of the cheese, then cover closely, and set aside until required.

3 Preheat the oven to 400°F. Grease a baking dish, and sprinkle with half the bread crumbs. Bring a saucepan of lightly salted water to a boil. Add the pasta, and cook for about 7 minutes or according to the instructions on the package.

4 When the pasta is just tender, drain it well, and return it to the clean pan. Reheat the sauce, add it to the pasta, and mix together until the pasta is completely coated. Spoon into the prepared dish, sprinkle with the rest of the grated cheese, and remaining bread crumbs, and bake for 20 minutes. Garnish with Italian parsley, and serve.

Pasta Napoletana

INGREDIENTS

1 pound mafalde or other dried pasta
basil sprigs, to garnish
freshly grated Parmesan cheese, to serve
NAPOLETANA SAUCE
2 tablespoons olive oil
1 onion, finely chopped
1 carrot, finely diced
1 celery stalk, finely diced
2 pounds ripe tomatoes or 2 x 14-ounce cans
chopped tomatoes
1 parsley sprig
pinch of superfine sugar
½ cup dry white wine (optional)
1 tablespoon chopped fresh oregano
salt and ground black pepper

SERVES 4

1 Start by making the sauce. Heat the olive oil in a saucepan, and add the onion, carrot and celery. Cook over a gentle heat for 5 minutes until the onion has softened but not colored.

2 If using fresh tomatoes, chop them coarsely with a sharp knife. Add the tomatoes (fresh or canned) to the pan, together with the parsley sprig, superfine sugar and wine (if using). Bring to a boil, lower the heat, and cook for 45 minutes until very thick, stirring occasionally.

3 Press the sauce through a strainer into a clean pan, or purée it in a food processor or blender, and strain it to remove the seeds. Add seasoning and oregano to taste, and reheat the sauce gently.

4 Bring a large saucepan of lightly salted water to a boil. Add the pasta, and cook for 10–12 minutes or according to the instructions on the package. Drain well, and toss with the sauce. Serve at once in heated bowls, topping each portion with the grated Parmesan cheese. Garnish with the basil.

Tortellini with Cream, Butter & Cheese

INGREDIENTS

¼ cup butter, plus extra for greasing
1¼ cups heavy cream
4 cups fresh tortellini
4 ounces Parmesan cheese in a piece
freshly grated nutmeg
salt and ground black pepper
fresh oregano, to garnish

SERVES 4–6

28

1 Grease a flameproof serving dish generously with butter. Bring a large saucepan of lightly salted water to a boil. Melt the butter in a separate pan, and stir in the cream. Bring to a boil, and cook for about 2–3 minutes, stirring until slightly thickened.

2 Cook the tortellini in the salted boiling water for about 3–5 minutes, or according to the instructions on the package, until it is *al dente*.

3 Grate all of the Parmesan cheese, and add three-quarters of it to the cream sauce. Stir the sauce frequently with a wooden spoon over a gentle heat,  until the cheese has melted. Add the salt, pepper and nutmeg to taste. Preheat the broiler to hot.

4 Drain the pasta, and spoon it into the dish. Pour the sauce over the top, and sprinkle with the rest of the cheese. Broil until golden, and garnish with oregano.

Baked Tortellini with Three Cheeses

INGREDIENTS

2 tablespoons butter
4 cups fresh tortellini
2 eggs
1½ cups ricotta or curd cheese
½ cup basil leaves, plus an extra sprig
to garnish
4 ounces smoked cheese (such as smoked
mozzarella or Cheddar), grated
4 tablespoons freshly grated Parmesan cheese
salt and ground black pepper

SERVES 4–6

1 Preheat the oven to 375°F. Grease a baking dish with the butter. Bring a large saucepan of lightly salted water to a boil. Add the tortellini, and cook for 3–5 minutes or according to the instructions on the package. Drain well.

2 Beat the eggs with the ricotta or curd cheese in a bowl. Add salt and pepper to taste. Spoon half of the tortellini into the prepared baking dish, then spread half of the the ricotta mixture over the top, and cover with half of the basil leaves.

3 Sprinkle with the smoked cheese and the remaining basil leaves. Top with the rest of the tortellini, and then spread the remaining ricotta mixture over the top.

4 Sprinkle evenly with the Parmesan cheese. Bake for 35–45 minutes or until golden brown and bubbling. Serve at once, garnished with basil.

Pasta Shells with Tomatoes & Arugula

INGREDIENTS

4 cups shells or other dried pasta shapes
3 tablespoons olive oil
1 pound ripe cherry tomatoes, halved
1 ½ cups fresh arugula leaves
salt and ground black pepper
freshly shaved Parmesan cheese, to serve

SERVES 4

2 Heat the oil in a large pan, add the cherry tomatoes, and cook for about 1 minute. They should only just be heated through and must not disintegrate.

3 When the pasta is just tender, drain it well, and add it to the tomatoes with the arugula. Toss gently to mix, taking care that the tomatoes do not break up. Season generously with salt and pepper. Serve immediately with plenty of shaved Parmesan.

1 Bring a large saucepan of lightly salted water to a boil. Add the pasta, and cook for 10–12 minutes or according to the instructions on the package.

COOK'S TIP

Use a swivel vegetable peeler to shave the Parmesan. If you haven't got a vegetable peeler, you could use a very sharp knife instead to produce fine shavings.

Simple Suppers

Spaghetti alla Carbonara

INGREDIENTS

6 ounces rindless unsmoked bacon
1 garlic clove, chopped
1 pound dried spaghetti
3 eggs, lightly beaten
4 tablespoons freshly grated Parmesan cheese
salt and ground black pepper
small parsley sprigs, to garnish

SERVES 4

3 When the pasta is just tender, drain it quickly, and add it to the saucepan containing the diced bacon and garlic. Stir in the lightly beaten eggs, a little salt, plenty  of ground black pepper and half the Parmesan cheese. Toss well to mix (the heat from the pasta will cook the eggs to a creamy coating consistency). Serve in heated bowls with the remaining cheese either sprinkled on top or presented separately in a small bowl. Garnish with parsley.

33

 I Using a sharp knife, dice the bacon, and place in a saucepan large enough to hold the cooked spaghetti. Heat gently until the bacon fat runs, then add the garlic. Raise the heat to moderate, and fry until the bacon is brown. Keep hot until required.

2 Bring a large saucepan of lightly salted water to a boil. Add the pasta, and cook for 10–12 minutes or according to the instructions on the package.

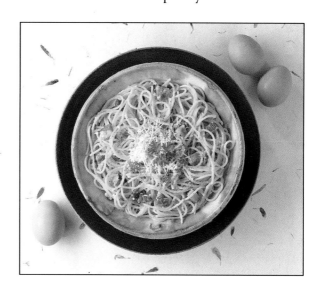

Penne with Eggplant & Mint Pesto

INGREDIENTS

*2 large eggplants, ends removed and cut
into short strips*
4 cups penne or other dried pasta shapes
*½ cup walnut halves, chopped, plus extra
to garnish*
MINT PESTO
½ cup fresh mint
¼ cup Italian parsley
scant ½ cup finely grated fresh Parmesan cheese
2 garlic cloves, coarsely chopped
6 tablespoons olive oil
salt and ground black pepper

SERVES 4

1 Layer the eggplant strips in a colander, strewing each layer with salt. Set aside to stand for 30 minutes over a plate to catch any juices. Rinse well in cold water, drain, and pat dry on paper towels.

2 Make the mint pesto. Combine the mint, parsley, Parmesan and garlic in a food processor or blender. Process the mixture until smooth. With the motor running, add the oil in a steady stream until the mixture forms a thick mayonnaise-style sauce. Add salt and pepper to taste.

3 Bring a large saucepan of lightly salted water to a boil, and add the dried pasta, then cook for about 8–10 minutes or according to the instructions on the package, until *al dente*. About 3 minutes before the pasta is cooked, add the eggplant to the pan. Stir together to mix well, and continue to boil in order to finish cooking the pasta.

4 Once the pasta is cooked, drain it along with the eggplant strips in a strainer or colander, then turn this mixture into a large bowl. Pour in half of the mint pesto and the chopped walnuts. Toss everything together well, and serve immediately, topped with the remaining pesto and walnut halves.

COOK'S TIP

Eggplants are available from all good supermarkets and grocery stores. They are either oblong or near-round in shape. Prime eggplants have a slight bloom to their shiny, tough skin; the meaty flesh is yellow-green.

Pasta with Traditional Pesto

INGREDIENTS

1 garlic clove, crushed
⅓ cup pine nuts
½ cup curd cheese
½ cup parsley sprigs
1 cup fresh basil leaves
2 tablespoons freshly grated Parmesan cheese
2 cups fusilli (twists) or other dried
pasta shapes
salt and ground black pepper
basil sprigs, to garnish

SERVES 4

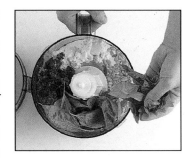

1 First make the pesto. Put the garlic, pine nuts and curd cheese in a food processor or blender. Add half the parsley sprigs and half the basil leaves, and process until smooth. Add the grated Parmesan cheese with the remaining parsley sprigs and basil leaves. Process until the herbs are finely chopped. Scrape the pesto into a bowl, add salt and pepper to taste, and set aside until required.

2 Bring a large saucepan of lightly salted water to a boil. Add the fusilli or other pasta shapes, and cook for 10–12 minutes or according to the instructions on the package.

3 When the pasta is just tender, drain it very well, return it to the clean pan, and add the pesto. Stir the pesto into the pasta taking care to make sure that all the pasta becomes fully coated. Serve in heated bowls, garnished with basil sprigs.

Tagliatelle with Sun-dried Tomatoes

INGREDIENTS

1 garlic clove, crushed
1 celery stalk, finely sliced
1 cup sun-dried tomatoes, finely chopped
6 tablespoons red wine
8 plum tomatoes, peeled and coarsely chopped,
or 14-ounce can plum tomatoes, chopped
12 ounces dried tagliatelle
salt and ground black pepper

SERVES 4

1 Combine the garlic, celery, sun-dried tomatoes and wine in a large saucepan. Cook over a gentle heat for 15 minutes. Add the chopped plum tomatoes,  and mix well. Add salt and pepper to taste, and let the sauce simmer while you cook the pasta.

2 Bring a large saucepan of lightly salted water to a boil, then add the pasta, and cook for about 10–12 minutes or according to the instructions on the package.

3 When the pasta is just tender, drain it well, and return it to the clean pan. Toss the pasta with half the sauce. Serve in heated bowls, topped with the remaining sauce.

37

Baked Vegetable Lasagne

INGREDIENTS

2 tablespoons olive oil
1 onion, very finely chopped
1¼ pounds tomatoes, chopped
or 2 x 14-ounce cans chopped tomatoes
6 tablespoons butter
1½ pounds mushrooms, thinly sliced
2 garlic cloves, crushed
juice of ½ lemon
4 cups béchamel sauce
4–6 tablespoons chopped fresh parsley
1½ cups freshly grated Parmesan cheese or
Cheddar, or a combination
12 sheets no pre-cook lasagne
salt and ground black pepper

SERVES 6–8

1 Preheat the oven to 400°F. Heat the oil in a saucepan. Add the onion, and cook for 10 minutes over a gentle heat until softened. Add the chopped tomatoes, and cook for 6–8 minutes, stirring frequently. Season with salt and pepper to taste, turn down the heat to the lowest setting, and simmer while you cook the mushrooms.

2 Melt half the butter in a frying pan, and cook the mushrooms for a few minutes. Add the garlic, lemon juice, and seasoning to taste. Raise the heat, and cook until the mushrooms start to brown. Meanwhile, stir the chopped parsley into the béchamel sauce.

3 Assemble the lasagne. Set aside about 3 tablespoons of the cheese for the topping. Spread a thin layer of the béchamel sauce in the bottom of a large, shallow baking dish. Cover with a layer of lasagne. Add half of the mushroom mixture, then add a few spoonfuls of the béchamel sauce along with a sprinkling of cheese. Top with another layer of lasagne, then half of the tomato mixture, then béchamel and cheese as before. Repeat these layers until all the ingredients have been used, finishing with a layer of pasta coated with béchamel. Sprinkle with the reserved grated cheese, and dot with the remaining butter. Bake for 30–40 minutes.

Pasta with Bolognese Sauce

INGREDIENTS

5 tablespoons butter
3 ounces pancetta or bacon in a piece, diced
1 onion, finely chopped
1 carrot, diced
1 celery stalk, finely chopped
8 ounces lean ground beef
½ cup chicken livers, trimmed and
coarsely chopped
2 tablespoons tomato paste
½ cup white wine
scant 1 cup beef broth or water
freshly grated nutmeg
1 pound dried tagliatelle or spaghetti
salt and ground black pepper
freshly grated Parmesan cheese, to serve

SERVES 4–6

1 Make the Bolognese sauce. Melt ¼ cup of the butter in a small saucepan. Add the diced bacon, and cook for 2–3 minutes until it starts to brown. Add the chopped onion, diced carrot and celery, and cook, stirring frequently, until browned.

2 Stir in the beef, and brown over a high heat. Stir in the livers, and cook for 2–3 minutes, then add the tomato paste, wine and broth or water. Mix well. Season to taste with nutmeg, salt and pepper.

3 Bring the sauce to a boil, lower the heat, and simmer for 35 minutes, stirring occasionally.

4 Bring a large pan of lightly salted water to a boil. Add the pasta, and cook for 10–12 minutes or according to the instructions on the package. Drain, return to the pan, and toss with the remaining butter. Spoon onto plates, and top each portion with some sauce. Serve with Parmesan cheese.

40

Pasta with Spinach & Anchovy Sauce

Ingredients

*2 pounds fresh spinach or 1¼ pounds frozen
leaf spinach, thawed
1 pound dried cappellini (angel hair pasta)
4 tablespoons olive oil
3 tablespoons pine nuts
2 garlic cloves, crushed
6 drained canned anchovy fillets, chopped
1 tablespoon butter*

Serves 4

I If using fresh spinach, remove any tough stalks, wash the leaves thoroughly, and place them in a pan with only the water that still clings to the leaves. Cover, and cook over a high heat, shaking the pan occasionally, until the spinach is just wilted and is still bright green. Drain. If using frozen spinach, simply drain it thoroughly, pressing out excess moisture. Cut the spinach leaves into strips.

2 Bring a large saucepan of lightly salted water to a boil. Add the pasta, and cook for 5–7 minutes or according to the instructions on the package.

3 Heat the oil in a saucepan, and fry the pine nuts until golden. Using a slotted spoon, transfer them to a bowl. Fry the garlic in the oil remaining in the pan until it turns pale golden. Add the drained anchovies and spinach to the pan, and continue to cook for 2–3 minutes or until the sauce is heated through. Stir in the pine nuts.

4 When the pasta is just tender, drain it well, pile it into a heated dish, and add the butter. Toss to coat. Pour the sauce over the top, fork it through roughly, and divide among individual heated serving dishes.

41

Pasta Salads

Tuna Pasta Salad

INGREDIENTS

*1 pound ruoti (wheels) or other dried
pasta shapes
4 tablespoons olive oil
2 x 7-ounce cans tuna in oil, drained
and flaked
2 x 14-ounce cans cannellini or borlotti
beans, drained
1 small red onion, thinly sliced
2 celery stalks, thinly sliced
juice of 1 lemon
2 tablespoons chopped fresh parsley
salt and ground black pepper
Italian parsley, to garnish*

SERVES 6–8

1 Bring a large saucepan of lightly salted water to a boil. Add the pasta, and cook for 10–12 minutes or according to the instructions on the package.

2 When the pasta is just tender, drain it well, rinse it under cold water, and drain again. Turn the pasta into a large bowl, add the olive oil, and toss to coat. Set aside to cool completely.

3 Add the flaked tuna, beans, onion and celery to the bowl with the cold pasta. Lightly toss together all the ingredients using a wooden spoon, until well mixed.

4 Mix the lemon juice with the parsley. Add to the salad, with salt and pepper to taste, and toss lightly. Cover, and allow to stand for at least 1 hour before serving, garnished with the Italian parsley.

43

Avocado, Tomato & Mozzarella Pasta Salad

INGREDIENTS

1½ cups farfalle (bows) or other dried
pasta shapes
6 ripe red tomatoes
8 ounces mozzarella cheese
1 large, ripe avocado
2 tablespoons pine nuts, toasted
1 basil sprig, to garnish
DRESSING
2 tablespoons wine vinegar
1 teaspoon balsamic vinegar (optional)
1 teaspoon whole-grain mustard
pinch of sugar
6 tablespoons olive oil
2 tablespoons shredded fresh basil
salt and ground black pepper

SERVES 4

1 Bring a large saucepan of lightly salted water to a boil. Add the pasta, and cook for about 10–12 minutes or according to the instructions on the package. Drain well, rinse under cold water, and drain again. Set aside to cool completely.

2 Using a sharp kitchen knife, slice the tomatoes and mozzarella into thin rounds. Cut the avocado in half, then remove the pit, and peel off the skin. Slice

the flesh lengthwise. Arrange the tomatoes, mozzarella and avocado around the rim of a flat plate, overlapping the slices evenly.

3 Make the dressing. Mix the wine vinegar and the balsamic vinegar, if using, in a bowl with the whole-grain mustard and sugar. Add a little salt and pepper to taste, then gradually whisk in the olive oil using a small whisk or a fork.

4 Add the shred-ded basil and half the dressing to the pasta. Toss well to coat. Pile the pasta onto the plate in the center of the avocado, tomato and mozzarella,

and drizzle with the remaining dressing. Sprinkle the pine nuts over the top, and garnish with the basil sprig. Serve at once.

Tomatoes with Pasta Stuffing

INGREDIENTS

8 large firm tomatoes
1 cup tiny dried pasta shapes for soup
8 black olives, pitted and finely chopped
3 tablespoons finely chopped mixed fresh herbs
4 tablespoons freshly grated Parmesan cheese
4 tablespoons olive oil
salt and ground black pepper
Italian parsley, to garnish

SERVES 4

1 Preheat the oven to 375°F. Slice the tops neatly off the tomatoes to serve as lids. Trim a thin slice off the bottom of any tomato which will not stand up straight. Scoop out the tomato pulp into a strainer, taking care not to break the shells. Stand the shells upside down on paper towels to drain, placing the lids next to them.

2 Bring a large saucepan of lightly salted water to a boil. Add the pasta, and cook for 2 minutes less than the time suggested on the package. Drain well, and turn into a bowl.

3 Add the olives, mixed herbs and Parmesan cheese to the bowl. Chop the drained tomato pulp, and stir into the mixture with the olive oil. Season with plenty of salt and pepper.

4 Using a large spoon, stuff the tomatoes with the filling, and replace the lids. Arrange the filled tomatoes in a single layer in a well-oiled baking dish. Bake in the oven for 15–20 minutes. Remove, and cool to room temperature. Serve with or without the lids, garnished with Italian parsley.

Whole Wheat Pasta Salad

INGREDIENTS

4 cups whole wheat fusilli (twists) or other
dried pasta shapes
3 tablespoons olive oil
2 small heads of broccoli, broken into tiny florets
1½ cups frozen peas
2 carrots, finely chopped
1 red or yellow bell pepper, seeded and chopped
2 celery stalks, thinly sliced
4 scallions, finely chopped
1 large tomato, diced
½ cup pitted black olives
1 cup diced Cheddar or mozzarella
cheese (optional)
Italian parsley, to garnish
DRESSING
3 tablespoons wine or balsamic vinegar,
or a 2:1 mixture
1 tablespoon Dijon mustard
1 tablespoon sesame seeds
2 teaspoons chopped mixed fresh herbs, such as
parsley, thyme and basil
4 tablespoons olive oil
salt and ground black pepper

SERVES 8

1 Bring a large saucepan of lightly salted water to a boil. Add the pasta, and cook for 10–12 minutes or according to the instructions on the package.

2 Drain the pasta well, rinse under cold water, and drain again. Turn into a large bowl, toss with the olive oil, and set aside to cool completely.

3 Boil the broccoli and peas until just tender. Refresh under cold water, and drain well. Add to the cold pasta with the carrots, pepper, celery, scallions, tomato and olives, and mix lightly.

4 Make the dressing by whisking the vinegar, mustard, sesame seeds and herbs in a bowl. Gradually whisk in the olive oil, then add salt and pepper to taste. Add the diced cheese to the salad, if using, pour over the dressing, and toss lightly. Cover, and allow to stand for 15 minutes before serving, garnished with Italian parsley.

47

Pasta Salad with Olives

INGREDIENTS

4 cups dried pasta shells
4 tablespoons extra virgin olive oil
10 sun-dried tomatoes, thinly sliced
2 tablespoons drained capers
⅔ cup black olives, pitted
2 garlic cloves, finely chopped
3 tablespoons balsamic vinegar
3 tablespoons chopped fresh parsley
salt and ground black pepper

SERVES 4–6

48

1 Bring a large saucepan of lightly salted water to a boil. Add the pasta, and cook for 10–12 minutes or according to the instructions on the package. Drain well, rinse under cold water, and drain again. Turn the pasta into a large mixing bowl, and add the olive oil. Toss together until the pasta is well coated, then set the pasta aside to cool completely.

2 Place the sun-dried tomatoes in a bowl, and pour a little hot water over them. Allow to soak for about 10 minutes, then drain, reserving the soaking liquid. Chop finely, and put in a bowl. Add the capers, black olives, garlic and balsamic vinegar.

3 Add the tomato mixture to the pasta, with seasoning to taste. Toss well. Add 2–3 tablespoons of the sun-dried tomato soaking water if the salad seems too dry. Toss with the parsley, cover, and set aside to stand for 15 minutes before serving.

Warm Pasta Salad with Ham, Egg & Asparagus

INGREDIENTS

1 pound asparagus spears, trimmed
1 small cooked potato, about 2 ounces, diced
5 tablespoons olive oil
1 tablespoon lemon juice
2 teaspoons Dijon mustard
½ cup vegetable broth
1 pound dried tagliatelle
8 ounces sliced cooked ham, ¼ inch thick, cut
into fingers
2 hard-boiled eggs, sliced
salt and ground black pepper
2 ounces fresh Parmesan cheese, shaved

SERVES 4

49

1 Cut each asparagus spear in half, and place the bottom halves in a pan of boiling salted water for 12 minutes. Remove with a slotted spoon to a colander, refresh under cold water, and drain.

2 Now add the asparagus tips to the pan of boiling water, and cook for 6 minutes. Drain, and refresh as for the thicker halves.

3 Roughly chop about 5 ounces of the thicker asparagus halves, place in a food processor or blender, and add the potato, oil, lemon juice, mustard and broth. Process to a smooth dressing. Pour into a pitcher, and add salt and pepper to taste.

4 Bring a large saucepan of lightly salted water to a boil. Add the pasta, and cook for 10–12 minutes or according to the instructions on the package. Drain  well, rinse under cold water, and drain again. Turn into a large bowl, add the asparagus dressing, and toss to mix. Spoon onto plates, topping each portion with ham, hard-boiled eggs and some cooked asparagus tips. Serve with shavings of Parmesan.

Mediterranean Salad with Basil

INGREDIENTS

2 cups penne rigate (ridged quills) or other
dried pasta shapes
6 ounces fine green beans, trimmed
2 large ripe tomatoes, sliced or quartered
1 cup basil leaves
7-ounce can tuna in oil, drained and flaked
2 hard-boiled eggs, sliced or quartered
2-ounce can anchovy fillets, drained
capers and black olives, to serve
DRESSING
2 tablespoons white wine vinegar
2 garlic cloves, crushed
½ teaspoon Dijon mustard
2 tablespoons shredded fresh basil
6 tablespoons extra virgin olive oil
salt and ground black pepper

SERVES 4

1 Make the dressing. Whisk the vinegar, garlic, mustard and basil in a small bowl. Gradually whisk in the olive oil, then add salt and pepper to taste.

2 Bring a large saucepan of lightly salted water to a boil. Add the pasta, and cook for 10–12 minutes or according to the instructions on the package. Drain well, rinse under cold water, and drain again. Turn into a bowl, add 2 tablespoons of the dressing, and toss to coat. Set aside to cool completely.

3 Bring a small saucepan of lightly salted water to a boil, and add the blanched beans. Blanch them for about 3 minutes so they are crisp to the bite. Remove from the heat, and drain, then refresh under cold water to prevent further cooking, and drain again.

4 Arrange the tomatoes in the bottom of a shallow salad bowl. Moisten with a little of the remaining dressing, and cover with a quarter of the basil leaves. Add the beans, in a neat layer, and moisten them with a little more dressing. Cover with a third of the remaining basil leaves.

5 Spoon the pasta into the bowl, cover with half the remaining basil leaves, and arrange the tuna and the hard-boiled eggs on the top. Finally sprinkle all the anchovies, capers and black olives over the salad. Drizzle the remaining dressing over the top, and garnish with the remaining basil leaves. Serve.

Easy Entertaining

Fettuccine with Saffron Mussels

INGREDIENTS

4–4½ pounds fresh mussels, scrubbed
and bearded
2 shallots, chopped
⅔ cup dry white wine
generous pinch of saffron strands
12 ounces dried fettuccine
2 tablespoons butter
2 garlic cloves, crushed
1 cup heavy cream
1 egg yolk
salt and ground black pepper
2 tablespoons chopped fresh parsley, to garnish

SERVES 4

53

1 Place the mussels in a large saucepan. Add the shallots and wine. Cover tightly, and cook over a high heat for 5–8 minutes, shaking the pan frequently, until the mussels have opened. Using a slotted spoon, remove the mussels from the pan. Discard any mussels that have not opened during the cooking process. Set aside a few of the mussels in their shells for garnishing; shell the rest, and keep them hot until required.

2 Bring the cooking liquid remaining in the saucepan to a boil. Cook until it has reduced by half, then strain it into a pitcher, stir in the saffron strands, and set aside.

3 Bring a large saucepan of lightly salted water to a boil. Add the pasta, and cook for 10–12 minutes or according to the instructions on the package.

4 Meanwhile melt the butter in a frying pan. Cook the garlic over a low heat for 1 minute, then pour in the saffron-flavored mussel liquid and the cream. Heat gently until the sauce starts to thicken, then remove the pan from the heat, and stir in the egg yolk and shelled mussels. Season to taste.

5 When tender, drain, and season the pasta, then divide among serving plates. Spoon over the sauce, and garnish with parsley and the reserved mussels.

Cannelloni al Forno

INGREDIENTS

1 tablespoon butter
1 pound boned and skinned chicken
breasts, cooked
8 ounces mushrooms, trimmed and halved
2 garlic cloves, crushed
2 tablespoons chopped fresh parsley
1 tablespoon chopped fresh tarragon
1 egg, beaten
lemon juice (see method)
12–18 dried cannelloni tubes
2½ cups Napoletana sauce
½ cup freshly grated Parmesan cheese
salt and ground black pepper
Italian parsley sprigs, to garnish

SERVES 4–6

1 Preheat the oven to 400°F. Using the butter, generously grease a large baking dish or a shallow casserole large enough to hold all the cannelloni in a single layer. Chop the chicken coarsely, then place it in a food processor fitted with a metal blade, and chop it very finely. Scrape into a mixing bowl, and set aside until required.

2 Add the mushrooms, garlic, parsley and tarragon to the food processor, and process finely. Add to the chicken, then stir in the egg. Season with salt and pepper, and add a dash or two of lemon juice.

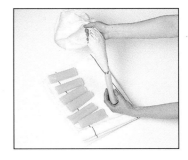

3 Cook the cannelloni in boiling water if necessary (check the instructions on the package), and drain well. Spoon the chicken mixture into a pastry bag fitted with a large plain nozzle, and fill the cannelloni tubes. Alternatively, fill the tubes with a spoon.

4 Put the tubes in the dish or casserole. Spoon over the sauce, and sprinkle with the cheese. Bake for 30 minutes, until golden. Garnish with parsley.

COOK'S TIP

Mushrooms are sold either as buttons, cups or flats according to age. Use mushrooms on the day of purchase as they don't store well — they go limp and lose their flavor quickly.

Tagliatelle with Gorgonzola Sauce

INGREDIENTS

1 pound dried tagliatelle
1 teaspoon cornstarch
2 tablespoons dry vermouth
2 tablespoons butter, plus extra for tossing
the pasta
8 ounces Gorgonzola cheese
⅔ cup heavy or whipping cream
1 tablespoon chopped fresh sage
salt and ground black pepper

SERVES 4

1 Bring a large saucepan of lightly salted water to a boil. Add the pasta, and cook for 10–12 minutes or according to the instructions on the package.

2 Mix the cornstarch with the vermouth in a cup. Melt the butter in a heavy-bottomed saucepan. Crumble in 6 ounces of the Gorgonzola, and stir over a very gentle heat until the cheese melts. Pour in the cream, then whisk in the cornstarch mixture. Stir in the sage, with salt and pepper to taste. Cook, whisking constantly, until the sauce thickens, then remove the pan from the heat.

3 When the pasta is tender, drain it, pile it into a large, heated dish, and toss in a knob of butter.

4 If it is necessary, reheat and whisk the sauce. Serve the pasta in heated bowls, topping each portion with sauce and the remaining cheese, crumbled on top.

Spaghetti with Seafood Sauce

INGREDIENTS

3 tablespoons olive oil
1 onion, chopped
1 garlic clove, crushed
8 ounces dried spaghetti
2½ cups strained, puréed canned tomatoes
1 tablespoon tomato paste
1 teaspoon dried oregano
1 bay leaf
1 teaspoon sugar
4 ounces cooked shrimp, peeled and deveined
1½ cups cooked clam meat (rinsed and drained
if canned or bottled)
1 tablespoon lemon juice
3 tablespoons chopped fresh parsley
2 tablespoons butter
salt and ground black pepper
4 whole cooked shrimp, to garnish (optional)

SERVES 4

1 Heat the oil in a saucepan. Add the onion and garlic. Cook over a moderate heat for 6–7 minutes, until the onion has softened.

2 Meanwhile bring a large saucepan of lightly salted water to a boil. Add the dried spaghetti, and cook for 10–12 minutes, or according to the instructions on the package, until it is *al dente*.

3 Stir the strained tomatoes into the onion. Add the tomato paste, oregano, bay leaf and sugar. Bring to a boil, then lower the heat, and simmer for about 2–3 minutes. Stir in the shellfish, lemon juice and two-thirds of the parsley. Cover, and then cook for 6–7 minutes. Season to taste.

4 When the spaghetti is just tender, drain it well, and return it to the clean pan. Add the butter, and toss until completely coated. Divide the spaghetti among four heated bowls, and top with the seafood sauce. Garnish with the remaining parsley and the whole shrimp, if using.

Shrimp with Pasta & Pesto in Packages

INGREDIENTS

1 ½ pounds whole medium raw shrimp
1 pound tagliatelle or similar pasta
⅔ cup fresh pesto sauce or pre-made equivalent
4 teaspoons olive oil
1 garlic clove, crushed
½ cup dry white wine
salt and ground black pepper

SERVES 4

1 Preheat the oven to 400°F. Twist the heads off the shrimp, and discard.

2 Cook the pasta in boiling salted water for only 2 minutes. Drain, and mix with half the pesto.

3 Cut four 12-inch squares of wax paper, and put 1 teaspoon olive oil in the center of each one. Pile equal amounts of the pasta mixture in the middle of each square.

4 Top each square with shrimp, and spoon the remaining pesto, mixed with the garlic, over the top. Season with pepper, and sprinkle the wine among them.

5 Brush the edges of the paper lightly with water, and bring them loosely up around the filling, twisting them tightly to enclose the filling.

6 Place the packages on a baking sheet, and bake for 10–15 minutes. Serve them immediately, allowing each person to open his or her pasta package.

COOK'S TIP
Try using other fresh fish and seafood instead of shrimp, if you prefer.

58

Linguine with Prosciutto & Parmesan

INGREDIENTS

4 ounces prosciutto
1 pound dried linguine
6 tablespoons butter
½ cup freshly grated Parmesan cheese
salt and ground black pepper
a few fresh sage leaves, to garnish

SERVES 4

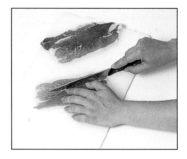

1 Using a sharp knife, cut the prosciutto into strips the same width as the linguine. Bring a large saucepan of lightly salted water to a boil. Add the linguine, and cook for 10–12 minutes, or according to the instructions on the package, until it is *al dente*.

2 Meanwhile melt the butter gently in a second small saucepan. Stir in all the prosciutto strips, and heat them through gently, taking care not to fry them.

3 When the linguine is ready, drain it well, then divide it among four individual heated serving plates. Sprinkle the Parmesan cheese over the top, then pour over the buttery prosciutto strips, and season with plenty of black pepper. (As the cheese is salty, salt need not be added.) Serve at once, garnished with the sage leaves. You may also like to serve this dish with some additional grated Parmesan cheese in a separate, small serving bowl.

Spaghetti with Black Olive & Mushroom Sauce

INGREDIENTS

1 tablespoon olive oil
1 garlic clove, chopped
8 ounces mushrooms, chopped
⅔ cups pitted black olives
2 tablespoons chopped fresh parsley
1 red chili, seeded and chopped
1 pound dried spaghetti
8 ounces cherry tomatoes
slivers of Parmesan cheese, to garnish

SERVES 4

1 Heat the oil in a large saucepan, and cook the garlic over a gentle heat for 1 minute. Add the mushrooms, raise the heat, and cover. Cook for about 5 minutes.

2 Turn the mushroom mixture into a food processor or blender. Add the olives, parsley and chili. Process until smooth, then scrape into a bowl, and set aside. Bring a large saucepan of lightly salted water to a boil. Add the spaghetti, and cook for 10–12 minutes, or according to the instructions on the package, until it is *al dente*.

3 Meanwhile heat an ungreased frying pan, add the cherry tomatoes, and shake the pan over a moderate heat for 2–3 minutes until the skins start to split.

4 Drain the pasta, return it to the clean pan, and add the olive mixture. Toss to coat. Serve the pasta topped with the tomatoes and garnished with the Parmesan.

61

Tagliatelle with Pea Sauce, Asparagus & Fava Beans

INGREDIENTS

1 tablespoon olive oil
1 garlic clove, crushed
6 scallions, thinly sliced
2 cups frozen peas, thawed
12 ounces young asparagus spears
2 tablespoons chopped fresh sage, plus extra
leaves to garnish
finely grated rind of 2 lemons
scant 2 cups vegetable broth
8 ounces frozen fava beans, thawed
1 pound dried tagliatelle
4 tablespoons plain yogurt
salt and ground black pepper

SERVES 4

2 Pinch the fava beans between your fingers to pop off the skins, revealing the tender green beans. Discard the skins. Bring a small pan of water to a boil. Cut the remaining asparagus into 2-inch lengths, add it to the boiling water, and cook until just tender. Drain well.

3 Bring a large pan of lightly salted water to a boil. Add the pasta, and cook for 10–12 minutes or according to the instructions on the package.

1 Heat the oil in a large pan. Add the garlic and scallions, and cook gently for about 2–3 minutes. Stir in the peas, and one-third of the asparagus, with the sage, lemon rind and broth or water. Simmer for 10 minutes, until the asparagus is tender. Purée in a food processor or blender until smooth, then return the sauce to the clean pan.

4 Add the cooked asparagus and the beans to the pea sauce. Stir in the yogurt, and reheat gently – do not allow the sauce to boil. Season with salt and pepper.

5 When the pasta is just tender, drain it well, and divide it among heated serving plates. Spoon the pea sauce over the pasta, garnish with some fresh sage, and serve at once.

62

Index